BOOKS BY ANN TAYLOR

Poetry:

The River Within
Bound Each to Each
Héloïse and Abélard: The Exquisite Truth
Sortings

Prose:

Watching Birds: Reflections on the Wing

Textbooks:

Short Model Essays
Shaping the Short Essay

LOOKING AFTER: POEMS

ANN TAYLOR

DOS MADRES

2024

DOS MADRES PRESS INC.
P.O. Box 294, Loveland, Ohio 45140
www.dosmadres.com   editor@dosmadres.com

Dos Madres is dedicated to the belief that the small press is essential
to the vitality of contemporary literature as a carrier of the new voice,
as well as the older, sometimes forgotten voices of the past. And in an
ever more virtual world, to the creation of fine books pleasing to the
eye and hand.

Dos Madres is named in honor of Vera Murphy and Libbie Hughes,
the "Dos Madres" whose contributions have made this press possible.

Dos Madres Press, Inc. is an Ohio Not For Profit Corporation and a
501 (c) (3) qualified public charity. Contributions are tax deductible.

Executive Editor: Robert J. Murphy

Illustration & Book Design: Elizabeth H. Murphy
www.illusionstudios.net

Typeset in Adobe Garamond Pro
ISBN 978-1-953252-98-2
Library of Congress Control Number: 2023951248

ACKNOWLEDGMENTS

My thanks to the editors of the following journals for publishing versions of these poems.

Sparks of Calliope, America's Main Street, Looking After (Taking Care); *The Galway Review*, I Couldn't Fathom Grace's Frost, Pandemic; *Copperfield Review,* Inside the Trojan Horse, Footprints, On Elephant Mountain, At Wounded Knee; *The Ekphrastic Review,* On the Aerodynamics of Angels, Benjamin West's Ben Franklin; *The Horn Pond Review,* Around the Pond, April 2020; *Portrait of New England,* Mount Washington, Late November; *Spitball,* The bases are filled with orioles!; *Appalachia,* Earliest Spring (Spring at the Pond), A Chittering of Juncos; *Lothlorien Poetry Journal,* Closed, Do Not Enter, Saint Kinga's Salt Chapel, Constellation Pegasus, Orders from Your Fairy Godmother

I would also like to thank my husband, Francis Blessington, and our children, Geoff and Julia, my Salem State students, plus the members of my Cambridge and Concord poetry workshops, guided by Tom Daley and Joan Houlihan.

For my grandson, James Francis Blessington

TABLE OF CONTENTS

I

II

III

IV

LOOKING AFTER: POEMS

To pay attention,
this is our endless and proper work.
—Mary Oliver

I

Oh, to cruise once more with them
this singular street

HOMESTEAD CLEARANCE

My mother was the best at it,
preferring blonde veneer and her own décor,
launching old tables, bedframes, wooden skis

out the attic window into a dump truck
backed beneath. I saw the china cabinet
with one cracked pane, go. But even she

held back, leaving in the attic
her father's barber shop scissors,
razors, bristleless brushes, her mother's

cut glass, red and white, one brother's
bent tennis racquet, the other's
business school texts and ice skates.

Also, her sister's backup sewing machine,
swatches of leftover fabric, and her own
collection of Infant of Prague robes.

In her studio, she left her ceramic molds,
paints, gilding, figurines with napkin skirts,
and my father's rocks, rods, and tackle.

Since my grandfather's 1890 move-in,
layers of lives settled here. What do I do
now with my father's ten-pin trophies,

my mother's hand-painted ceramic reindeer
with the blinking red nose? How much space
must I allow for so much life?

REACHING FOR THE SKY

Like manic stick figures
      in a Broadway extravaganza,
they danced and twirled across
      every neighborhood roof,
bent, thin limbs beckoning
      to one another and to open air.

I worried when my father joined
      that high-line chorus,
sidled across the tiles
      arm-in-arm with his antenna,
guaranteed to deliver the wide world
      without snow or ghosts.

When a noisy crow perched
      on an outstretched silver arm,
I dashed inside for a TV close-up, twisted
      the rabbit ears in all directions –
just a spectral ripple coursing
      through a twelve-inch blizzard.

AMERICA'S MAIN STREET

On three-hundred-mile car days,
the water in our portable
window AC hotter
than the summer blaze,
my sister and I whining
for a pool – any small oval
dug in the rough before a rustic motorcourt,
screen doors slamming in the wind,
outhouses at the rear.

Our always new,
pastel-with-white-striped De Soto,
yearly cruising Route 66 –
ruler-flat horizons, infinite cornfields,
stormy vistas, Triptik detours,
Burma Shaves, plywood jackrabbits,
trading-post temptations
like *baby rattlers,*
knotty pine everything.

Soaring over it all,
the *flying horsepower*
of the Mobilgas red Pegasus.

Those rattlers, a dusty scattering
of plastic baby rattles in a cage,
casting doubt on our genuine arrowheads
carved by the braves themselves
and on our authentic fossils
and gold nuggets.

My mother saving for, planning
those neon-lit, carhop, stalagtite,
teepee weeks, and my father,
the only driver, delivering us
to all of it.

Oh, to cruise once more with them
this singular street, to thank them
for that roadwise, wide-range awakening.

DETECTORIST OF THE HARDPAN

My father's a silhouette in late summer sunset,
pacing the beach, headphones in place,
swinging the flat head of his detector
with a steady rhythm broken
only when he pauses to shove his
spade in deep.

A banker by day, he trains tellers
to spot thieves, takes the stand
against crooks, but his off-duty heart
quests for buried treasure
free for his keeping –

as yet no chalices, torcs, nuggets,
no Spanish doubloons, but rusty toy cars,
tin soldiers, loose change, belt buckles
and bottlecaps, and once, framed in gold,
a cameo brooch for my mother,
the creamy profile polished smooth.

In the backyard, he shows me
his newest detector, with sharper
hearing, longlife battery.
Coming up with nothing
in his scoured lawn, he plants
a coin in the grass himself –
Listen to this!

A storm forecast, he's eager
to pace the next day's roiled sand,
but this night, his unreliable heart
fails him, his powered-up machine
propped at the door.

I COULDN'T FATHOM GRACE'S FROST

She skipped her son's wedding,
and later offered only
her cheek for me,
her eldest grandchild, to kiss.

Ringed on hard chairs in her kitchen,
the family teased out Sunday
after-Mass conversation,
as Buzzy, the housecat, prowled
unfriendly among our feet.

Into my teens, I had grown wintry
myself with her, and at her funeral,
wished to speed up the soprano.

I glanced at my father beside me,
saw him wipe his wire-rimmed glasses,
as a tear worked down his cheek.

When I patted the back of his hand,
I surprised myself with a tear –
the closest I ever came to warmth
for her, and that not even my own.

ATLANTIC CITY *THRILL RIDE*

My mother got me to the Steel Pier early,
but I was too small in the crowd
to follow the whole leap.
I heard the splash-landing.

I did see the horse climbing the ramp
and the girl mounted bareback
leaping into the air from the tall tower –
the blur of the rider riding low
like a jockey, the horse looking
so out of place, tail lifting in the wind.
I heard my mother shout, *That poor horse!*

Less impressed with *Rex,*
the Water-skiing Wonder Dog
and the *Boxing Kangaroos,*
I begged for her to return
to the *Thrill Ride* for a better view
at the night show. I failed.

That day's sharpest memory
remains the one-inch streak of blood
on my mother's cheek, scratched there
by herself as she tried too quickly
to cover her eyes.

SHE MADE THE SINGER SING

From a custom-cut, pinned
mound of slipcover fabric,
Aunt Mary could stitch
a couch in an hour –
backpanels, skirts, arm pieces,
all aligned with the beasts,
plants, patterns, tales in the cloth.

Chatting with me,
her inexpert cord-cutter,
she roared the foot-treadle motor,
drew out the emerging couch
with the speedy industrial needle,
tried to make me
her stitcher's apprentice.

Drawn by her patience
and her ease with the Singer,
I too tried, but feared
the drag of that drive.
Safer, I ironed, then folded
her work for delivery.

Hating now my peeling faux-leather
couch, I long for a custom slipcover,
maybe with a Renaissance scroll.

I wish for her to be here,
trying to guide my fumbling fingers,
(and maybe whipping up a couch for me).

LOOKING AFTER

The white-haired custodian
helps me with hauling my hi-fi
to my second-floor apartment –

a studio, with one door
and a window too high
for jumping.

At the second landing, he gestures
me to the window. *Come take a look.*
Down there. On a cement slab,

a man in powder-blue sweater lies
face-down, arms spread into wings,
legs buckled backwards.

The cops think he jumped from up there.
I step back. *Nothing to be afraid of*
. . . only a dead body.

I've just traded my unlocked
family house for a dim hallway
of numbered doors, chain-bolt rattles.

And my futon, lobster trap table,
Chianti-basket candle holders,
Night Hawks in the kitchenette

fail to make here a home.
Then Sven delivers from his stash
in the basement, four glass blocks

to hold up my door desk,
I thought they'd work,
and switches on my gooseneck lamp.

Knowing he and his wife
dwell just beneath me,
among pressed cottage curtains,

cream cakes, and Hummels,
I brave the rickety back staircase
from my car, sleep better.

All summer, he places orange cones
in my space behind the building,
shoos away Red Sox fans. *They'll park*

in your living room, if you don't
lock your door, and without a word,
sweeps bottle glass

from his immaculate front steps,
trashed by my out-of-hand
student party the night before.

Later that night, he taps on my door,
jingles the keys left outside in my lock.
Thought you might need these.

SLOW LEARNING

You just don't understand!
my mother protested.

Hearing, seeing, keeping up,
simply holding her balance
on the altar step – the takeaways
of my mother's years
into her nineties.

She's too unsteady for those steps,
the pastor said, *We don't want her to fall.*

Her car taken, she waited at her window
for her friend to drive her to breakfast
with the old altar crew,
after they finished their work.

No private ceramic studio,
thrift shop sales, no good-will visits
to the lonely ones at the re-hab.
Only the exhaustion of waiting
for the good will of others.

I don't want to be a burden,
she'd repeat, *I hate to bother people.*

No bother, my breezy reply.

Before accumulating years of my own
and one broken ankle, before COVID's
cruel disengagements, I argued back:
I do understand.

I didn't.

WALTZING

I cheered for *Ice Capades* kick lines,
      Olympic leaps and spins,
barrel-jumpers, clowns, but as a young teen,
      I loved the septuagenarian waltzers,
the *Old Smoothies,* the best.

I loved her sequined sparkle rippling
      in the chilly air, and his all-white
tuxedo and tails, lifting on their turns,
      I loved their glide, as one,
across the shining ice,
      every swerve and twirl spotlit.

Only once so far,
      with a boyfriend's senior uncle,
had I danced
      with such shared ease and grace.
Just relax, he said,
      I'll do the leading. And he did.

One hand firm on my back,
      the other a gentle grip,
we one-two-three'd the entire floor,
      floating forward, so light of foot
my saddle shoes might be skates.

With their effortless sweep
      of ice, air, light, the *Smoothies*
drew me from the acrobatics
      and the antics, spun me
back to the rush
      of that startling dance.

ARE THEY YOURS?

Wrong mother! says my son's
second grade classmate,
alarmed I'm kidnapping him.
No, his skintones and my Irish pale
don't match, but since days after his birth,
I've been the right mother.

One hand to her heart,
the other patting my daughter's head,
the Florentine *nonna* announces,
Hai un cuore grande,
Were my Italian better,
I would offer my set response
to this undeserved praise –
No, it's my gratitude,
not my big heart.

Are they brother and sister?
asks the mother of five screamers
in the circus ticket-line.
They are now! my usual dodge
from that nosy question.
Mom goes on,
Do they know their parents?

Hoping to share the delights
of adoption, I bring both kids
to the agency's gathering
for potential parents
where the director focuses on my son

vrooming his plastic frontloader
across the living room. She points,
This one is typical.

I flinch. No, not *typical,*
not a sample kid, but his unique self,
hoisting a stuffed bear into a bucket.

As we three exit that show-and-tell,
one possible parent declares,
*Oh, my God, I hope they realize
how lucky they are!*

ROOT CANAL

He whistles *Jingle Bells,*
promises a *tiny pinch,*
my grip on the chair tighter
than a launching astronaut's.

Suddenly, the comforting
tedium of the beige wall,
Latin degrees,
amateur painting
of the too-blue stream
riffling through the evergreen
mountain pass – all flash
to pure snowwhite on white.

I wrench my head aside,
try to sit up, bite down.
Guess we need
a little more novocaine,
he murmurs.

For the first and last time,
my silent companion,
with me since teething,
my own dishonored nerve,
demands attention,
resists oblivion.

RECURRING DREAM

I ascend the podium,
settle my sheets,
raise my arms
above the orchestra –
the harmonies all mine.

My wand hand-glides
through air, calls up
the pianist and woodwinds
beckoning to the rumbling bass,
the harp rippling at the fringe,
the soprano awaiting my sign –
a masterpiece,
        but this time the snare-drum
resists the score, insists
        on extended vibration.

The flute purrs
as-planned *pianissimo,*
        but my platform buckles

as my cat pokes me off the podium –
        Classic Seafood Paté,
subito . . . prestissimo.

CLASSES OVER

cellphones the focus,
college-hall swerves to exit --
echolocation.

NIGHT-TALK

Sleeping with the radio on is not a good idea,
warns a health website, and may cause
shaky equilibrium, loss of hearing,
depression, cancer, death.

Not enough for me to silence
my voices in the night, for years eased
into childhood sleep by my father, mother,
and aunt chatting at the kitchen table,
just outside my bedroom door.

Then teen transistor radio –
Top 40 countdowns,
Elvis vs. Pat disputes, and years later,
into the night of my own apartment,
my clock radio gabbing Boston restaurants,
visiting in-town acts, antique books.

Testing, I tune out my night-chat for a while,
but raindops, crickets, white noise,
the sheep, the silence, keep me awake.

Now, through a padded speaker pressed
beneath my pillow, newshounds, psychics,
trivia experts keep the world awake for me,
while I drift off with Morpheus.

SUNLIGHT AND SHADOWS: EIGHT MONTHS

He's learned that his hands
are all his, that his voice can be
called upon at will, that a smile
elicits smiles, much hand-clapping.

Today it's sunlight's lessons.
Circled in a bright spot
on the rug, he works
to grasp the lit-up flowers,
slaps hard enough to de-petal them,
calls them strange sounds.

It's the shadows this time,
moving with him, responding
to every gesture – his raised hand,
the wild swing, that shady other baby
crawling with him.

Deliberate, he moves, stops, stares,
stays still for any sign of life,
laughs when the shadow
waves back – a happy haunting
this time.

II

For the literary life of you,
don't ever forget whatever it was
that held you so enchanted

ORDERS FROM YOUR FAIRY GODMOTHER

Fetch your flashlight, hide again
under your blanket,
your earliest castle built
just for you and the words.

Help Gretel stoke up her oven,
fan the flame. Shut down
the witch's cackles. Cheer
her incineration.

Cry with the bullied duckling,
punish his tormentors,
exclude them from the party
so they feel what it's like.

Shiver when the hungry wolf huffs
at the pigs' unsturdy doors. Applaud
Pig Three. Clap when the big windbag
gets stymied.

Hop a fairy-dust ride in your pumpkin
chariot. Savor Cindy's sweet revenge.
Dance when the shoe fits
and she marries the handsome one.

Do not overstudy Hansel's eating habits,
pity the witch's wicked heritage,
or question the innocent beauty
of the swan's white feathers.

For the literary life of you,
don't ever forget whatever it was
that held you so enchanted
in your secret flashlight glow.

TAKEN BY TROLLS

by the cute ones at Oslo shops,
with horned helmets, bulbed noses,
dumbo ears, lumpy feet, They jig
on coffee cups and lampshades,
play the violin, bake cookies,
grin at customers,

by the less endearing in the tales,
with weedy hair, tree-trunk limbs,
touchy tempers. They kidnap babies,
gnaw at the moon, devour cows whole,
and Christians.

And by shape-shifting ones,
secreted in cliffs, lurking in greenery,
but easily spotted from boats, tourvans,
private cars. They hurl wild stones
at intruders, and at dawn turn themselves
into boulders strewn across the landscape.

Yes, let's stay here!
my friendly bobblehead
dashboard troll nods,
but I reject the fairy cottage,
woodcarved hearts, windowboxes,
and the outhouse outside,
nestled too deep in shade.

I choose the inn with private bath
and breakfast room panorama window –
a wide-angle rubble of stones
all the way to the cliff base,
and right in front of my car,
a very large boulder – I'm sure
not there when I pulled in.

INTRO. TO ASTRONOMY

Orion reliably hunting the winter sky,
        Pegasus galloping, Leo launched
into the heavens by Hercules –
        once familiar asterisms, consoling tales,
but their shapes, alas, still shifting.

The astrophysicist, the whirling simulations,
        Morgan Freeman's YOUtube spacetour
all saying that thirteen and a half billion years ago,
        a pinpoint of pressure big-banged
matter, energy, space, time, into being –
        all of us therefore stardust.

A trip around the world no trip at all,
        our sun equalling one million earths.

Four hundred billion stars just in our Milky Way,
        among *trillions of galaxies,*
counting dizzying *septillions of stars.*

Supernovas, white dwarfs, quasars exploding,
        black holes *spaghettifying* us should we
near the void where light can't shine.

Leaving my night class, an ever-keener
        pinpoint of pressure in my brain,
trying to remember where on earth I parked my car.

CONSTELLATION PEGASUS

For bearing his thunderbolts,
Zeus stellified his stallion
in truth, more a celestial dishevelment,
than a heavenly horse,
leaving it for tale-tellers
to finish the picture –

his divine birth
from Poseidon's godly foam
and dying Medusa's blood,
his hoofed-up watersprings
on Helicon, invoking poetry
from rock,

his soaring with Bellerophon
on his back to kill the lion-headed,
snake-tailed Chimera,
then bucking him off,
for the hubris of spurring him
too near the heights of Olympus.

Zeus left his *Great White* steed
as an upside-down half-a-horse
with two rickety legs,
a probable neck, maybe a muzzle,
but still a stallion open
to gallop across the night sky,
strong enough to carry his stories.

INSIDE THE TROJAN HORSE

Odysseus' *elite*, we thirty, crammed
full-armed into a huge horse-womb,
wobbly on wooden wheels,
a stray whisper sure to betray us.

Rough respite, after a decade
of storming, laddering impossible walls,
cascading back to our blood-drenched tents.

We fear to hear, close between the planks,
Laocoön's wise distrust
of our oversized battlegift, but then
suddenly no more from him.

Stench mixing with wood-scent suffocation,
we shiver, try to settle, as our spirits
sink. Odysseus wags his sword
side to side into a *No!* glares us
into bracing our spines.

We freeze when Cassandra names our deceit
straight on – the horse, the plot, the death –
Nonsense! they determine. We exhale,

ache for an exit, wait for this beast
to be trundled through the gate, eager,
no matter the cost, to free ourselves
from this splintery nightmare.

ILIUM TRANSPORT

The haywagon, donkey-drawn,
delivers us by gravel path
across Achilles' campsite
to Priam's Troy, to where
the laden horse once paused
before its fatal rolling in,

and where the boy driver buckles
the rig into a sharp u-turn,
shouts *Allahaismarladik*, a blessing,
and nods to our *Güle güle*,
the polite good-bye
he taught us on the way,

just as we turn to Homer's war zone,
retrace the tale of slaughter, fallen towers,
vengeance, brave Hector's death
his body dragged, chariot-bound,
his head defiled in dust,

and Achilles' iron heart, finally transformed
from war-rage to simple mercy, giving back
to Priam his son's anointed body,
himself lifting Hector onto the polished
mule-wagon for secure delivery
across the merciless battlefield.

FOOTPRINTS

The Laetoli trail says
        two walkers,
one large, one smaller,
        maybe a third,
smaller still, marched tall,
        across the savanna,
upright, with a straight-ahead
        heel-strike, toe-off gait.

It must have rained
        and rained
that day three and a half
        million years ago,
during the eruption,
        and molded forever
into sodden ash
        their seventy steps.

Where were they heading?
        Away from the firestorm?
A predator?
        To the shelter
of distant greenery?
        To a neighbor's kill?

Were they drawn
        to a sharp turn ahead?
Or were they simply
        out for a stroll,
at last soaking in
        the sulky sun after days
of choking ashfall?

BIFACE HANDAXE
IN THE METROPOLITAN ART GALLERY, 370

Did he crouch at the dark's woodfire,
just outside the cave's mouth?
Was he busy, his rough tools

chipping, grinding this ten-inch
honey-colored flintshape,
sharp-edged, serviceable
for everyday hunting, butchering,
severing, scraping of hides?

Predators for a while at bay,
did he draw a callused finger gentle
along its tapered symmetry?

Was his eye caught by ivory veins
laced delicate through
this hewed layering?
Was he moved for a time
beyond coarse necessity?

In the gallery, miles and millenia ahead,
it's featured straight up,
commanding attention.

SERMONS CARVED IN STONE

All Seven Deadlies, like the *Covetous*
with the money bags too heavy to lift,
the *Wrathful* punching a foe almost off

their tiny platform. And too the devil
gnawing the sinner's cheek. The skeleton
devouring the woman's skull –

all there in dusty cathedral corners,
on the high tops of capitals,
in niches to the side of the winding stair –

eternal damnation. Here too, sculptors
brightened the Dark Ages with acrobats,
bagpipers, dancers, mischievous monkeys,

readers literally curled up with a book,
and yes, men defecating from on high,
mooners mooning, contorted matings.

The sculptor's task was to terrorize
with hellish visions, but the imp in him
must've smiled at his vulgar nose-picker,

forever leaning out from a tall column,
hovering just above a very busy,
sanctified side aisle.

ON THE AERODYNAMICS OF ANGELS

Draped in weighty earth-tones,
DaVinci's Gabriel kneels
in this walled garden,
casts a deep shadow
across the lawn
of blooming flowers.

Straight from heaven,
he delivers his message
to Mary, who turns
from her book,
welcomes him.

Not at all the usual
floating illumination,
this angel is grounded.

The scientist, so exact
about mechanical workings
of everything, leaves
his angel's celestial wings
unfit to hoist his heft
even an inch into air.

Flying, Gabriel
is equipped to soar
with a single wingstroke,
to all places, all at once,
but descended to earth,
bearing worldly news,
he's unmistakably,
for the moment, like us.

CLOSED, DO NOT ENTER

The Glastonbury graves visited,
the Tor climbed, but the iron gate

to the holy Chalice Well –
denied, padlocked –

the final resting place of
the Last Supper cup,

cup raised at the crucifixion
to collect sweat and blood

from Christ's five wounds,
flowing deep red in sympathy,

cup carried in procession
through the candled throne room

of the crippled Fisher King
able to cure his injury,

cup, holiest of all,
the San Graal of King Arthur's

court, earned by Galahad
for his purity of heart,

cup given by Christ himself
to Joseph of Arimathea,

who bore it straight to England,
placed it in this redwater well,

the cup that compelled us that day
to climb up and over the gate.

DEFLECTION

Behind the newsflash body
draped dead on the sidewalk,
I look for an escape, imagine
chatting masons busy there
one hot summer day –
a made-up scene, a turnaway.

At the base of a Naples slope,
I drive through the torrent
forcing trash barrels, plastic chairs,
into my bumper, threatening to take over
my steering, but the flashing red
APERTO in the window of the pizzeria
calms me down.

When the thriller killer stalks
the terrified girl, I think of her
as silly in a silly plot, remind myself
of the crew in the cobwebby basement
beside her – director, sound
and camera staff, and especially,
the gaffer with the lights.

But no matter how eagerly
I concoct a better view,
my devious efforts allow me
no lasting way out.

I too must descend,
unaccompanied,
into the downstairs dark

ON ELEPHANT MOUNTAIN

Screws and studs still lined up neat
across B52 Stratofortess surfaces
intact, painted, shiny,
as they were meant to be,

      before the stabilizer gave way,
    stole all control in the storm,
before seven crewmen died
      in the mountain's thick greenery.

Buckled, twisted, and burnt
    metal six miles in,
      along the Maine woodpath.
A six-foot wingshape wedges high
      in the crook of a maple limb.

It's quiet, without the steely rampage
of a large plane shredding fir
      and hardwood forest,
        grounding all parts of itself.

Small American flags flutter
      from the fuselage.
      Against a frayed, blown tire
      a cracked passenger window leans
where it never should be.

SAINT KINGA'S SALT CHAPEL

At the head of the nave,
a salt altar enshrines
my unworthy remains.
Here I reflect on my
once uncrystallized,
unsainted life.

I yearned only to be a singular
whisper down a candled convent hall
and out to a cloister garden beneath
the Creator's sky uncircumscribed.

But fashioned a queen, a saint,
I must spirit this salt shrine,
mined in my honor,
where salt chandeliers glitter for me
and salt-frescoed walls tell my story.

At the base of this deep shaft,
my statue stands, my salt robe etched
in scrolls, my hair laced pretty
about my face, my crown faceted.

A miner carved of salt
kneels before me, offers
a ring encased in a salt
crystal block.

I want neither ring, nor rock,
just a way out to earth dew-softened,
the caress of air chilled
or thawed with the seasons —
heaven's reward.

THE SAME *STILL, SAD MUSIC*

English major's seminar rooms,
whale-road kennings done for the day,
I escape down Comm. Ave.
to honkey-tonk Hillbilly Ranch.

I leave Milton's devils, cursing
with hellfire/To waste his whole creation,
then pray with the Lilley Brothers'
to *Drop kick me Jesus*
through the goalposts of life.

Keats' *fade far away* sad nightingale
prepares me for Hank Williams' grief,
also shared by a bird,
Did you ever see a robin weep
when leaves begin to die?

Charlie Waller's deathwish
to come back as a song
yearns, like Emily, for lasting consolation –
'Tis sweet to know that stocks will stand/
when we with Daisies lie.

And too Ozymandias' *half sunk,*
shattered visage in the desert,
foreshadows John Lincoln Wright's
Hillbilly elegy, the Ranch's neon
Schlitz signs gone to rubble,
broken windows black and blank,
when the wreckin' ball blew it away.

III

I'll watch until it depart
on its double set of wings.

ROWDY OF THE MEADOW

At the top of a hayfield stalk,
one bobolink, black and white,
formal with yellow crown cap,
trilling deep-down organ tones –
a chorus, Emily says,
Too intimate with Joy,
enough to lure her
from the Sabbath's
Presbyterian birds.

Birders try to mime the song –
Tom Noodle, Tom Noodle, you owe me,
or *spink, spank, spink,* or *bobolink.*
Then there's the ambitious,
puck puck pi, deedla eh ah, eeee-ew, d-t-d-t dee.
Nobody gets it right.

In spite of cats in the grass,
angry spring plows,
her *Bird of Birds* sings its own
bobolink medley, resists
predictable melody, inspires
swagger for her songs,
her own *sentiments seditious.*

A CHITTERING OF JUNCOS

On a frosted maple limb,
the hawk puffs up

against the chill wind,
watches their avalanching,

digging snow craters
for seed dropped from the feeder

by the locals. Wind spirals
drifts about them.

Lead sky above, snow below,
the bird books say,

their black and white
top-to-bottom snowbird

coloring, like the day itself —
horizon tamped down

to earth, snow ridged
across the cutting edge.

Too at home here,
too at ease.

WILD-WESTING

Spin off your office chair.
       Abandon the soft-eyed,
huggable Lab puppy screen,
       and trot west,
to wind-whipped grains,
       dessicated, fenceless desert,
deer and antelopes' rough rumbling.

       Skip *parameters,*
operating procedures,
       metaconferences,
and, securely mounted,
       race open space,
ford angry rivers,
       chase down a tumbling
tumbleweed, stare
       eye-to-eye at varmints
trapped in its prickly roll
       across the plain,

Back from your happy trail,
       again encubicled,
you may then post
       a more authentic,
up-to-date screen shot –
       a peering-from-the-thorns,
googly-eyed-tongue-flicking,
       clawed, horned lizard.

PONY EXPRESS

Must Be Lightweight, Willing to Risk Death Daily. Orphans preferred.
—California job listing, 1860

Mochila stuffed with five-dollar mail
      and ten-day-old news,
I was a lone one, eager to prod
      my ponies into ten-mile laps
for seventy-five miles, day or night –
      through desert, blizzard,
robbery, tomahawk ambush,
      forever seduced by sleep –
taking my own deathrisks
      until the telegraph outran me,
delivered me to *spectacle*
      Wild West, where I spurred
a dust-choked circle,
      faked relay landings and leaps,
fought feathered warriors
      hired to throw daily battles,
until the mob's mockery
      told me I was done here,
and so, with a final slap,
      I released my mount to the hills,
envied that mustang's snort,
      the toss of his mane, the fade
of his four-beat gallop away.

TURTLES

follow the warm up our coast
   where they thrive the summer,
until descending cold stuns them
   into lethargy, drains
all power to lift a head,
   oar a flipper, become
strandends in the embrace
   of Cape Cod Bay,
where the wind drives
   them to the beach,
and where heat comes
   from rescuers
who provide blankets,
   warmer and warmer water tanks
and maybe a charter flight
   south where healing
allows them to swim back
   into the north's summer embrace.

ALL AT ONCE

on an Arkansas New Year's Eve,
redwinged blackbirds
plummet by thousands,
dangle like broken ornaments,
twist in shrubbery, sprawl
across pavement. Breeze stirs
the only wing-flutter.
Epaulets rust.

Rousted from their roosts
into coarse collision
with unwelcoming night –
frightened, unforgiven,
they're at last broomed
into undifferentiated heaps.

This spring, the vanguard arrives
here, all shiny black and fire-red,
riding high on cattails,
trilling *koorees,* calling for
the fulness of the breeding flock.
All the more welcomed this year,

EARLIEST SPRING

The sodden log rocks, lazes
on wavelets, worries duckweed,
with six turtles, painted in a row,
raised high, lolling warm and dry.

Then the one log-rolling coot,
unbalances, disturbs the peace,
tips them into clawscrambling
their hold above the muddy murk.

Un-iced, sun sprung, a warbler trill,
a louder cardinal call, log-and-turtle rest,
coot dance, my long pause on the trail –
the season's wakenings.

THE MAPLE

The summer crew beheads
        my neighbor's tree,
splays disassembled limbs, stacks
        ring-years to dry in the sun.

For decades, a neighborhood canopy,
        the home-tree for *Hide and Seek*
and cap-pistol shoot-outs,
        its rough bark the safe base.

Later, a presider over snowmen
        armed with maple twigs. And too,
deep shade for generations
        of grown-up Adirondacks.

No comfort knowing the tree was
        theirs, not ours, not mine. No joy
in sunlight for that new grass,
        only resistance to the new sky view.

GULL

Redness splays from the bill
and bibbs down the breast
of a young Herring Gull.
In the bleak winter harbor,
he looks almost spruced up,
his ascot formal, but with binoculars,
I see it's a spongy slab of red plastic.

Bill forced open, he jerks his head
back and forth, up and down,
coughs, chest-heaves,
slams the red into the water.

I reach for my throat,
want to dive in, hope
one of his wrenchings
will dislodge his gagging.
Colliding with a dockpost,
he shakes his head,
bobbs in the water.

A quick swallow,
this red must've seemed a prize
won by finishing first.

DO NOT FEED

At the roadside pullout,
one looks like roadkill,
splays out flat.
Another's an oval,
like a punch-me inflatable.

The bottom-heaviest tips
over, off balance, scrambles
in the dust to get up.

Instinct should tell all prairie dogs
to rise tall on their mounds,
the better to hear the look-out's
bark, warning of snake, fox, hawk.

But these charming townies,
with practiced eye-contact,
prayerful paws pressed
in begging, await treats
strewn about them
like confetti – Cheerios,
half-eaten granolas,
carrots, silver kisses.

Here among foot-tall
DO NOT orders red-painted
on the pavement,

a kid coaxes,
Over here, little prairie dog!
casts wide a fistful of Smartfood.

DARWIN PLAYED THE BASSOON
FOR HIS BACKYARD EARTHWORMS

before joining them, he said.
He breathed on them, served them
onions, cabbages, cherries to study
their diet, noted their indifference
to piano melody.

In his seventies, he hoped
to prove that they too
possess some degree of intelligence.

He reveled in their *perception of luminosity,*
and observed that *their sexual passion
is strong enough to overcome for a time
their dread of light.* They impressed him
when they purposely dragged leaves
across their burrow entrances,
in nearly the same manner as would a man.

He knew they *stood low —*
deaf, mostly blind, unable to smell,
but for their dogged renewal of the soil
he thought *we ought to be grateful.*

His own life so simplified,
he wished to be buried in the familiar soil
of St. Mary's churchyard,
near his house of forty years,
and by his children's graves —
the sweetest place on earth.

To honor his worldly achievements,
they moved him from his own rich turf
to Westminster's north choir aisle
entombed among the greats –
beneath a Carrara marble paving stone.

PANDEMIC

Mountain goats plod
dusty village plots,
lions lounge
the hunters' trail,
their cubs frolicking.
Kangaroos window-shop
Main Street stores –
pandemic soft news.

Harsher, a preview
of our time here done at last –
mailboxes buckled
before abandoned houses,
city limits blended
with open fields,
steeples grounded,
lights dim, like us –
all reclaimed by wind,
water, too much warmth.

Just outside the weathered front door,
twisted on its broken hinges.
an over-fed bobcat
sprawls the length
of a garden magnolia limb,
yawns toothily.

AROUND THE POND, APRIL 2020

On my route around the pond,
I veer an arc, as a masked hiker
passes, arms extended wide
to assure empty space around him.

Less off-putting with one another,
early redwings gather among the cattails,
Old Sam Peabody sparrows
convene in the mulberry bush,
and from a low pine branch,
the *Who Cooks for You?* Owl speaks.

A solo snapper crowds in
for sunning on an already
well-turtled log,
while whole companies
of migrating geese descend,
honk an immediate departure,
driven off by one cranky swan,
wings slapping the surface
into a foam.

Except for the swan,
who relishes all stay-away orders,
there's not much distancing.
Turtles line up to sun,
birds congregate promiscuously,
travel without permission,
chorus openly.

On my walk, I spy
from the lagoon bridge
the elusive Wood Duck,
a painter's palette of Spring color
emerging briefly from the reeds.

But must resist my urge
to summon others in close,
to share with me
this passing delight.

WHERE IS THE ENTRANCE TO THE RUIN?

This COVID year, no Lyon *coq au vin,*
Norse sailing ship, Kenyan ostrich-race,
No *How old is that banyan?*
Or, *Is that koala smiling at me?*

Now it's the pond's creature life
deep in shadow waiting
for me to match up
in my nature guides.

So too the swamp-pond birds I've missed
and the bugs, swatted up to now,
anonymous, unappreciated.

Gilbert White loved his village swifts,
bats, mice, perspiring trees,
and Timothy, his mopey tortoise.
He loved close-up views –
The fossil shells of this district,
and sorts of stone which have fallen
within my observation
must not be passed over in silence.

And after world travel, Darwin was taken
by his own worms' behavior patterns,
focusing on their response to vibrations –
Earthworms also remained quiet
when placed on a table near a piano.

So, I'll devote a whole day
to my shrubs, a week
for stone rubble in my garden,
and I'll identify the winding vine
prying my house drainpipe
from its bracket, before I kill it.

Today, on my front step, I discover
a grapevine beetle, elegant,
about an inch long, tan-colored
with four black spots running down
each side, its legs and eyes dark black –
a true *Pelidnota punctata* of the family
Scarabaedae. I'll watch until it departs
on its double set of wings. Exotic.

HAILSTONES

hard-boiled-sized stones

      drive to ground in gusts,

merge under white

      the graves of Wild Bill

and Calamity Jane,

      and at the State Fair, drive

Tigger, Elmo, Elsa

      straight down the midway,

where barkers try to pluck

      their plush prizes

from slush puddles.

      And at the park, hail pounds

staccato on bison heads,

      calves skurry skiddy trails

to their mothers,

and prairie dogs burrow

themselves. We shelter

in our rental van, getting

pounded, pockmarked,

hood to trunk.

MOUNT WASHINGTON, LATE NOVEMBER

A casual stroll up the paved road
for the view we never get to see.

Freezing fog turning everything
rimey, prickle-white –

the stiffening of tree-limbs,
low greenery, logs flat out, us.

Crystal spikes crackling
the only sound around,

except for the skid and slide
of the wrong footwear descending.

THE GENTLEMAN'S SPORT

Trained for fight and fury,
      lethal with ankle-blade spurs,
Cock Number 87 highsteps
      the *valla*, a mini-bullring,
where bettors shout bids
      on his chance for life
five minutes from now
      against *Number 91,*
whose handler lifts him,
      forces his beak into *87's,*
provokes wrath, drops him
      to the sand where they clash,
orange-ruffled, lion-maned,
      a flurry of feathers,
until *87* rises high,
      slashes, blade first,
blasts an explosion
      of yellow, red, gold,
until *91's* wing splays,
      head lolls too long
on the sand, so handlers
      raise them both again,
thrust them again
      into one another,

the attacks weaker now,
      as *87* launches down
and down to clamp finally
      on *91*'s bent beak,
then through a slurry
      of sand, feather, blood
struts victory.
      Next up, a caged cock crows,
raucous enough to rouse
      a country mile.

THE BASES ARE FILLED WITH ORIOLES!

announces the color commentator
this April afternoon – a pretty picture
all orange, black, and lively,
the greensward rolling to the wall.

But not the view of the spoiler
in the red socks, whose sole aim
is to muddy those birds up,
clip their wings, force them back
fast to their dim digs,
tarred with sunflower shells,
chew, and spit.

Today, he freezes their flight
to home, throws them all out.

His next mission?
To chill the red-hot bluejays
winging from Toronto.

IV

No extra hand to count
the seconds
where time is simply done.

ALCATRAZ CLOCK

Ringed with imperial
        numerals on white,
a twelve-inch circle
        high on the wall
above a sign naming
        this dull dining hall
TIMES SQUARE.

No tourist scramble,
        stage curtain calls,
falling ball glittering
        revelers into the new year.

Just the mess-line shuffle
        of current *irredeemables,*
ghosts of the past trailing them,
        brief swipes of sky,
tide's enticement,
        rhythmic on the rock,
XX minutes of *pass the bread,*
        before the shuffle back
to long-drawn celltime.

Stalled in place,
        hours proceed.
No extra hand to count
        the seconds
where time is simply done.

DON STOVER, DOING HIS POST-HILLBILLY BEST

This out-of-town room's a tough one,
gagging in smoke, the boozy crowd
shouting for pitcher refills, starting up
the rock jukebox as soon as Don and the boys
take a breather for a cigarette and
Station I-drinkification.

A few of us Hillbilly migrants cheer
for his overdrive *Foggy Mountain,*
and quick *Fox on the Run,*
but in this banjo-dead zone,
Don must work to jolly the audience,

*This song makes me feel better
all over more than anyplace else!*

Or, *I opened the refrigerator
the other night and heard a shout,*
CLOSE THE DOOR! WE'RE DRESSING!

He tries *Cripple Creek,*
picks and sings three sets for the pay.

At closing time, it's spotty applause
as he finishes his own composition,
Things in Life, lamenting those things
life takes away from us

and ending with a wish
that when he dies,
You can say I done my best.

SITTING BULL

When his sundance vision
foresees the defeat of Army soldiers
falling like grasshoppers from the sky,
he sparks his braves to bloody victory
at Little Big Horn.

Behind him in Buffalo Bill's sideshow,
his fake-tomahawk warriors parade,
lose mock battles to mock settlers,
then stand aside when fans line up
to shell out two dollars
for his celebrity autograph.

Posing all puffed up beside him,
Bill himself is smitten, calling him
a wonderful old fighting man,
his beaded, bossy eagle feathers
cascading from the top of his head
to his moccasins.

At the end, his ghost-dancers
whirl in a circle for days,
drum ancestors back to battle,
stir fatal fears of another Big Horn.

Lakota Tatanka Iotanka,
soldier, showman, shaman,
the chief.

AT WOUNDED KNEE

Today, persistent gusts
scorch the hill to the graves,
where chain link embraces
the burial trench and multi-colored,
weathered ribbons stir in the wind.
Dry grass rattles.

Beside the memorial signpost,
a Lakota mother offers
for sale a hand-webbed,
feathered dreamcatcher
made by her daughter.
In the wind, it spins.

WILD BILL'S DEADWOOD

Rally cycles all chromed up,
riders all leathered,
Old Glory pressed on jeans,
biker-beards competitive –
spade-shaped, forked, braided –
and the gals too in leather,
silver studs, and chains,
red bandanas, hugging
drivers from the rear seat,
speakers blaring above the growl
of bikes, hundreds of thousands
convened in one place.

It's possible to toe down Main
across saddle seats to Saloon #10's
mounted deerhide heads
of legendary locals, black and white
glossies of Bill, and hovering
above the door
in a red velvet showcase,
his death chair,
toasted by the bikers.

BENJAMIN WEST'S BEN FRANKLIN

Red, black, gold oil on slate,
draped in stormy robe,
face glowing in skylight,
his hero looks up,
ascends beyond the inches
of his small picture frame.

Boots solid on airy cloud,
he's a near-apotheosis.
Designer of everyday
hearth-stove, bi-focals
and swim flippers,
this Ben's superhuman
raised among angelic putti
holding taut his kite string,
monitoring his vial and rod,
enticing electricity.

Not as lofty as the Sistine's
heavenly finger-strike
between Father and Son,
but Ben's bent knuckle
reaches high too
for a spark of power,
his key ignited.

SCOFFER'S ADVICE

I'm thrown under the bus,
        by some dope dumping
the blame on me,
        but I outlast the roar,
pavement scrapes,
        engine rattle, deathly fumes,
while below the LimoLiner
        contoured seats, Wi-Fi, A/C
I cling to the greasy axel,
        nudge reluctantly over
for the others rolling
        regularly in, hold on tight
up to the next red light,
        where I slip out from under,
track down that thrower
        himself who'll conclude
he should've thrown me
        in front of.

AUTUMN, MY LAST YEAR OF TEACHING DONE

Again this year, I watch ash leaves
fray first, withdraw from the left.
From the right, maples, wind-thinned,
pull aside like curtains, open the familiar
vista from pines to causeway bridge,
from ice house landing to mountain.

After months of leaf-muffled noise,
Canada geese reliably call out clear,
paddle sunrippled water, countable.
A squirrel stocks with fallen leaves
the drey swaying among high limbs,
while crows mob the redtail no longer
hidden deep in shadow.

Nothing at all new.
The difference all in me.

GOOSE-PASSING

Watering my draggled-by-drought flowers,
I hear above my head the September honking,

expect a leader in the lead, advancing
the V-vanguard to he landing. But not today.

This one, with no one behind or beside,
wings on, disengaged, but persistent,

still feeling the urge to guide others
through autumn's resistant air.

NOTES

Atlantic City Thrill Ride: from 1928 to 1978, Atlantic City's Steel Pier featured mounted horses high-diving off forty foot platforms.

Waltzing: The Old Smoothies, Irma Thomas and Orrin Markhus, skated ball-room style during the 40's and 50's.

Footprints: Laetoli is a paleontological site in Tanzania, where in 1976 Mary Leakey discovered footprints in volcanic ash. Dated 3.7 million years ago, the footprints are evidence of early, bi-pedal humans.

On the Aerodynamics of Angels: Leonardo Da Vinci's, *Annunciation* (c1472), at Florence's Uffizi, portrays this visitation.

Closed, Do Not Enter: Joseph of Arimathea is said to have placed the holy chalice in the Chalice Well in Glastonbury, England.

On Elephant Mountain: The 1963 mountain crash site is a short distance from Maine's Moosehead Lake.

Saint Kinga's Salt Chapel: About to be married to a Polish prince, the Hungarian Princess, Kinga, knowing the importance of salt in Poland, requests salt as her dowry. She later throws into a local mine shaft her engagement ring that is later dug up in Poland in a block of salt. She becomes forever the patroness of Polish salt miners. The Wielicza Salt Mine Chapel is carved in her honor.

Pony Express: An express mail service that operated between Missouri and California from April,1860 to October, 1861. Buffalo Bill Cody (1846-1917), founded the Wild West Show in 1883. It continued on for thirty years.

All At Once: In Beebe, Arkansas, December 31, 2010, 3,000 to 5,000 blackbirds died.

Where is the entrance to the ruin? Gilbert White (1720-1793) the "parson naturalist," wrote a detailed *The Natural History of Selborne.*

Hailstones: Wild Bill Hickok and Calamity Jane are buried side by side in the Mount Moriah Cemetery near Deadwood, South Dakota.

Don Stover, Doing His Post-Hillbilly Best: Don Stover (1928-1996), singer, composer, banjo player, entertained Bostonians with Bluegrass music during eighteen years at the Hillbilly Ranch.

Sitting Bull: Born in 1831 and died in 1890, he was a leader of the Sioux resistance to the advancement of white settlements.

At Wounded Knee: Site in South Dakota where on December 29, 1890, 300 Lakota people were killed by U.S. Army soldiers.

About the Author
ANN TAYLOR

A long-time Professor of English at Salem State University in Massachusetts, Ann Taylor has written two books on college composition, academic and free-lance essays, and a collection of personal essays, *Watching Birds: Reflections on the Wing*. Her first poetry book, *The River Within*, won first prize in the 2011 Cathlamet Poetry competition at Ravenna Press. A chapbook, *Bound Each to Each*, was published in 2013. Her collection, *Héloïse and Abélard: the Exquisite Truth*, published in 2018, is based on the twelfth-century story of their lives, and her most recent collection, *Sortings*, was published by Dos Madres Press, in 2020. She is currently at work on a collection of poems focusing on Horn Pond in Woburn, Massachusetts (*Horn Pond: The Way I See It*), near which she grew up and where she now lives again.

OTHER BOOKS BY ANN TAYLOR
PUBLISHED BY DOS MADRES PRESS

SORTINGS (2020)

FOR THE FULL DOS MADRES PRESS CATALOG:
www.dosmadres.com

www.ingramcontent.com/pod-product-compliance
Lightning Source LLC
Chambersburg PA
CBHW031219120626
46545CB00003B/908